ANIMAL KINGDOM CLASSIFICATION

SPONGES, JELLYFISH & OTHER
SIMPLE ANIMALS

BY STEVE PARKER

CONTENT ADVISER: LEONARD MUSCATINE, PH.D.,
EMERITUS PROFESSOR OF BIOLOGY,
UNIVERSITY OF CALIFORNIA, LOS ANGELES

SCIENCE ADVISER: TERRENCE E. YOUNG JR., M.ED., M.L.S.,
JEFFERSON (LOUISIANA) PUBLIC SCHOOL SYSTEM

First published in the United States in 2006 by
Compass Point Books
3109 West 50th St., #115
Minneapolis, MN 55410

ANIMAL KINGDOM CLASSIFICATION–SIMPLE ANIMALS
was produced by

David West Children's Books
7 Princeton Court
55 Felsham Road
London SW15 1AZ

Designer: David West
Editors: Gail Bushnell, Anthony Wacholtz, Kate Newport
Page Production: James Mackey

Visit Compass Point Books on the Internet at
www.compasspointbooks.com
or e-mail your request to
custserv@compasspointbooks.com

Library of Congress Cataloging-in-Publication Data
Parker, Steve.
  Sponges, jellyfish & other simple animals / by Steve Parker.
     p. cm.—(Animal kingdom classification)
  Includes bibliographical references.
  ISBN 0-7565-1614-5 (hardcover)
  1. Invertebrates—Juvenile literature. 2. Sponges—Juvenile
literature. 3. Jellyfishes—Juvenile literature. I. Title: Sponges,
jellyfish, and other simple animals. II. Title. III. Series.
   QL362.4.P367 2006
   592—dc22   2005029183

PHOTO CREDITS :
Abbreviations: t-top, m-middle, b-bottom, r-right,
l-left, c-center.

Title page, OAR/National Undersea Research Program (NURP);
8t, OAR/National Undersea Research Program (NURP); 8b,
Florida Keys National Marine Sanctuary; 9m, OAR/National
Undersea Research Program (NURP); 9br, Oxford Scientific
Films; 10, Florida Keys National Marine Sanctuary; 11l, NOAA;
11r, NOAA; 12, Oxford Scientific Films; 13t, Oxford Scientific
Films; 14l, Oxford Scientific Films; 15r, OAR/National Undersea
Research Program (NURP); 15b, Dr. James P. McVey, NOAA;
16/17, Florida Keys National Marine Sanctuary; 17t, OAR/
National Undersea Research Program (NURP); 17b, Oxford
Scientific Films; 18/19, Kip Evans, NOAA; 20l, Captain Albert
E. Theberg, NOAA; 20/21, Kip Evans, NOAA; 21t, Oxford
Scientific Films; 21m, Oxford Scientific Films; 21b, NOAA;
22l, Oxford Scientific Films; 22/23, Oxford Scientific Films;
23t, OAR/National Undersea Research Program (NURP);
23b, Oxford Scientific Films; 24l, Oxford Scientific Films; 25t,
Kip Evans, NOAA; 25b, OAR/National Undersea Research
Program (NURP); 26t, Oxford Scientific Films; 26b, Florida
Keys National Marine Sanctuary; 27tl, OAR/National Undersea
Research Program (NURP); 27b, Dr. James P. McVey, NOAA;
29m, Oxford Scientific Films; 30t, Dr. James P. McVey, NOAA;
30b, Richard B. Mieremet, NOAA; 31m, Oxford Scientific
Films; 31b, Emma Hickerson, NOAA; 33t, Dr. James P. McVey,
NOAA; 34t, Erik Zobrist, NOAA Restoration Center; 34/35,
NOAA; 35t, OAR/National Undersea Research Program
(NURP); 35b, Dr. James P. McVey, NOAA; 36b, OAR/National
Undersea Research Program (NURP); 37l, OAR/National
Undersea Research Program (NURP); 37r, Oxford Scientific
Films; 38l, Oxford Scientific Films; 38/39, Dr. James P. McVey,
NOAA; 39l, Oxford Scientific Films; 39r, Oxford Scientific
Films; 40/41, Oxford Scientific Films (all); 42, Oxford Scientific
Films;

With special thanks to the models: Felix Blom,
Tucker Bryant, and Margaux Monfared.

Front cover: Tube anemone
Opposite: Bell jellyfish

SPONGES, JELLYFISH & OTHER
SIMPLE ANIMALS

Steve Parker

COMPASS POINT BOOKS MINNEAPOLIS, MINNESOTA

TABLE OF CONTENTS

INTRODUCTION

Some animals are complicated, both in their bodies and their behavior. Parrots, dolphins, chimps, and dogs have hundreds of body parts and exhibit behavior that relies on thought processes. Compared to them, many other creatures are "simple." This is because, in general, they have fewer kinds of body parts and their actions are far less complicated.

But "simple" does not mean they are unsuccessful. Many simple creatures are thousands or even millions of times more common than more complex ones.

Most of these simple creatures live in the ocean and are less familiar to us than land animals. Yet they are some of the most fascinating, beautiful, and bizarre of all living things. They help us to explain how creatures of all kinds began during prehistory, hundreds of millions of years ago. And like other wildlife today, they also suffer from modern dangers such as pollution and global warming.

AMAZING COLORS, FANTASTIC SHAPES
Sponges and corals hardly seem alive—they are some of the world's simplest creatures. Yet over hundreds of years, they gradually construct reefs far larger than anything people have built—reefs that are homes to endless varieties of marine life.

DIVERSE AND NUMEROUS

Almost no living place on Earth is free from simple creatures. Different kinds can thrive where bigger, more complex animals with more specialized needs would soon perish.

WATERY WORLDS

Most simple creatures live in water. This includes the world's biggest main habitat—the ocean. Many simple animals have jellylike bodies that would soon dry out if exposed to air. Water keeps them wet and supports their floppy parts.

Some simple creatures have a limited ability to move. In fact, some are fixed to the same place through almost their entire lives. Again, water is helpful—it can bring food to stuck-down sponges. The food might be tiny floating bits of plants and animals or microscopic plants and creatures called plankton. Water can carry jellyfish long distances to new feeding areas, and provide meals for anemones, who grasp and sting passing fish or shrimps.

WORLDS WITHIN WATER

The main habitat of the oceans is really a collection of many different places. They vary from the wide-open water to sunny tropical shallows, waves pounding on rocky shores, ripples on sandy beaches, tides lapping across mudflats, ice-covered polar seas, and the cold blackness of the depths. Different kinds of simple creatures are suited, or adapted, to all of these surroundings—and more.

OPEN WATERS
Siphonophores

SHALLOW SEASHORES
Sea squirts

SUNLIT TROPICS
Coral

SHALLOW AND DEEP SEA BEDS
Sponges

UNDERWATER CURRENTS
Jellyfish

TIDAL ZONES
Anemones

EVEN SIMPLER LIFE

Animals, including simple ones, are living things whose bodies are made of many microscopic "building blocks" called cells. Animals also get their energy and nutrients by taking in, or eating, food and then digesting it (breaking it down) inside their bodies. In these features, animals differ from other kingdoms, or huge groups, of living things.
• Members of the plant kingdom get their energy from sunlight.
• Members of the fungus kingdom break down food outside their own bodies.
• Members of the protist kingdom, like amoebas, are not many-celled but unicellular—one cell each.

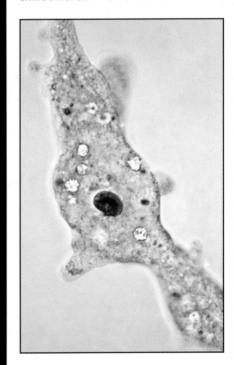

Amoebas live in fresh water.

INSIDE A SIMPLE ANIMAL

Simple animals lack bones, a brain, a heart, and even blood, which many animals have inside their bodies. They do not have eyes, ears, teeth, or joints. While they have few parts, simple animals come in a variety of shapes.

BODY PLANS

Many simple animals have very simple body plans. There are parts to gather food, and there are parts to digest food. Food varies from things like small particles for sponges to larger prey for jellyfish. Digestion parts are usually like bags or containers. The other key feature of living things is reproduction. Simple animals all have body parts for breeding.

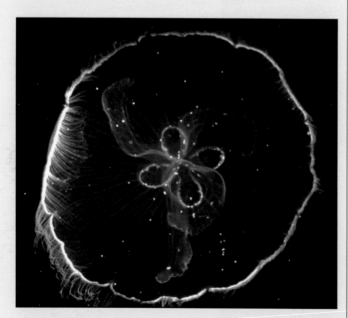

SEE-THROUGH SIMPLICITY

This moon jellyfish has four curved pouchlike guts and four breeding parts forming a central cross inside its main body or bell.

SPONGE

A basic sponge is like a stiff jar or vase. Water carrying tiny bits of food is sucked in through many small side holes and flows out through one main hole.

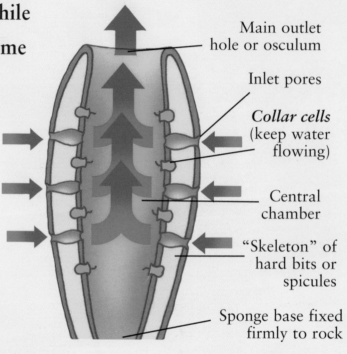

Main outlet hole or osculum

Inlet pores

Collar cells (keep water flowing)

Central chamber

"Skeleton" of hard bits or spicules

Sponge base fixed firmly to rock

JELLYFISH

The main body of the jellyfish can move because of a ring of muscles around its edge. The mouth where food goes in is also the anus where leftovers come out.

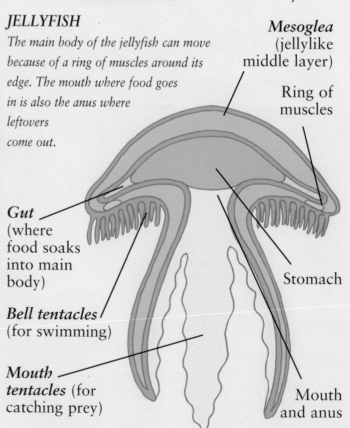

Mesoglea (jellylike middle layer)

Ring of muscles

Gut (where food soaks into main body)

Stomach

Bell tentacles (for swimming)

Mouth tentacles (for catching prey)

Mouth and anus

ANEMONE

The sea anemone is like an upside-down jellyfish. It has tentacles to catch prey, and a central mouth that leads to the stomach in its stalk.

Tentacles
These curl around prey and are covered with thousands of tiny stingers (below right).

Mouth
As in the jellyfish, the anemone's mouth is the way in for fresh food and the way out for digested leftovers.

Stalk
This contains the main stomach chamber and simple guts, and the breeding parts.

SIMILAR BUT DIFFERENT

From the outside, sea squirts look similar to sponges. They live on rocks, and have a baglike body with a hole at the top. But closer study shows that sea squirts have two holes (siphons), incurrent and excurrent, and they are more flexible and leathery than sponges. Also a sea squirt has more complicated parts inside its body, including nerves and muscles, which sponges lack.

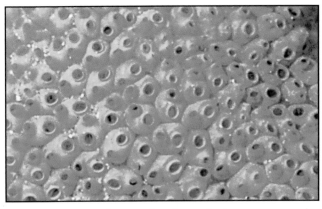

Some sea squirts live in closely packed groups.

ANEMONE'S STINGERS

Each stinger, or nematocyst, is a single cell, far too small to see. If something touches the hair trigger, the micro-sting flicks out with tiny barbs that grab and stab poison into the victim.

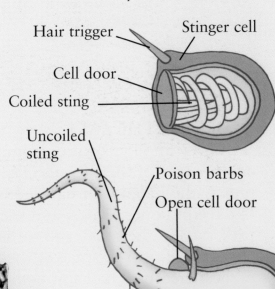

Hair trigger — Stinger cell

Cell door

Coiled sting

Uncoiled sting

Poison barbs

Open cell door

ORIGINS OF SIMPLE ANIMALS

More than 600 million years ago, simple animals were the first creatures on Earth, when life could only be found in the sea. There are still many mysteries to uncover about their beginnings.

FOSSIL SPONGE

Many different kinds of fossil sponge have been found in the Wenlock Hills of Southern England. This species of Raphidonema found there dates back to the Cretaceous era, 115 million years ago.

CLUES TO THE PAST

We know about creatures from long ago because of their fossils. These are mostly the remains of hard body parts like teeth, bones, claws, and shells, preserved in the rocks and turned to stone. However, some of the very earliest creatures had soft bodies. Their fossils are faint and rare, and tell us little about their size and shape.

PLENTIFUL REMAINS

One main group of simple creatures that left fossils are the sponges. Their hard, sometimes stony bodies were often well preserved. These fossils show that sponges were very similar to those alive today. They lived in the seas, filtering small bits of food from the water.

FAMILIAR SCENE?

This view could almost be from today, with jellyfish drifting past and different shaped sponges and corals rising from the seabed. Yet it is from the Cambrian Period of more than 500 million years ago. The main difference is the lack of fish, which had not yet evolved.

1 *Sponge*
2 *Coral*
3 *Bryozoan colony*
4 *Brachiopods*
5 *Jellyfish*

FOSSIL CORAL

This coral, Kodonophyllum truncatum, lived in the warm seas of the Silurian era, over 420 million years ago. Each polyp's soft tissue tentacles can be seen folded into their hard shell.

A LONG HISTORY

Tiny coral animals also evolved well over 500 million years ago. Fossils of their small, soft bodies are scarce. However, bits of the huge rocky reefs they built have been preserved in great detail. Over millions of years, as other creatures like dinosaurs came and went, simple creatures, such as sponges and coral animals, hardly changed at all.

SUDDEN DEATH

Occasionally in prehistoric times, huge numbers of plants and animals suddenly died out, perhaps because of worldwide volcanic eruptions. Each of these mass extinctions was followed by a burst of change or evolution, as new kinds of life appeared. But simple animals survived all these mass extinctions.

Volcanos may have caused mass extinctions.

13

NO BRAIN SUCCESSES

The simplest of all simple animals are sponges. They cannot move about or sense their surroundings like most other creatures. But they "eat" and digest food, which makes them members of the animal kingdom.

Water comes out of the sponge's hollow body through a large hole, the osculum. Sponges are often covered with other sea creatures, like these small white anemones.

The bodies of many sponges contain spicules—microscopic spikes, rods, plates, and other shapes of hard mineral substances. Spicules make the sponge hard and stiff and sometimes prickly.

SPIKY "SKELETON"

The basic sponge body plan is a hard, stiff container, shaped like a vase or tube. The middle layer of a sponge's body, between its tough outer covering and inner lining, forms its "skeleton." It is a thick jelly containing tiny spikes or spicules of minerals, made from calcium (limestone) or silica. Some sponges also have strong fibers or threads mixed with the spicules.

IN AND OUT

Seawater is drawn into the sponge's body through many small holes, by thousands of microscopic cells in the sponge's inner lining. These cells are called collar cells or choanocytes. They have tiny "hairs" known as flagella. The flagella wave to and fro like tiny oars to keep the water flowing. A sponge often grows where there are natural water currents to help move the flow of water through its body.

SPONGE SUPPORT

Sponges can be like hills or trees on land. They are good places for fish and other creatures to rest and keep watch for food or danger.

HOW SPONGES FEED

The collar cells catch tiny bits of floating food, such as microscopic plants and plankton, or pieces of broken plants or animals. Then other microscopic cells, called amoebocytes, collect the pieces and ooze or "crawl" through the sponge's body, spreading the food.

HELPFUL PLANTS

Sponges' bodies are often home to other living things, including tiny plants. The plants catch sunlight energy and use raw materials provided by the sponge to grow. In return, the tiny plants make nutrients for the sponge in addition to its normal food. Many corals also have plant "partners" living on or inside them.

GREEN GLOW

This sponge's green color is caused by the tiny helpful plants living inside it. The sponge-plant partnership only works in shallow or clear water, where there is enough light for the plants.

SPONGES ON THE MOVE

Some sponges move around, but not under their own power. Most cannot even bend their bodies. Some live attached to shellfish like whelks and other sea snails. Others grow on the snail shell in which a hermit crab hides, or on the backs of crabs and lobsters. The sponge gets plenty of water to filter for food, and its animal partner gets protection and disguise.

Sponge crab with its "hat"

SPONGE SHAPES AND SIZES

The smallest sponges only grow to be the size of the dot on this "i." The biggest are larger than an adult human. Sponges also vary in shape, from round balls to long tubes and branching fans.

THOUSANDS OF KINDS

Sponges make up the major animal group, or phylum, called Porifera. Within this group are more than 5,000 different species, or kinds, of sponges. Each has its own shape, size, and color. However, these features alter depending on water temperature, current speed, and where the sponge lives. This means that members of the same species can look very different.

TUBE SPONGES

This group of tube or column sponges has grown up from a small area on a seabed rock. But each has its own separate body.

VARIED SHAPES

Some sponges have branching upright bodies like trees. Others grow flat on the rocks, like blankets. Sponges are often named after well-known objects, like barrels.

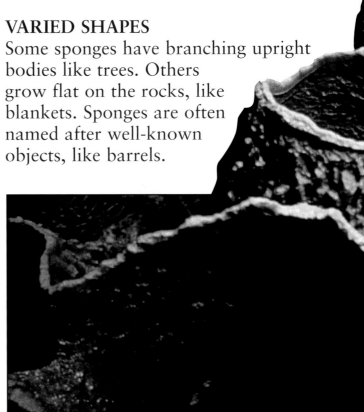

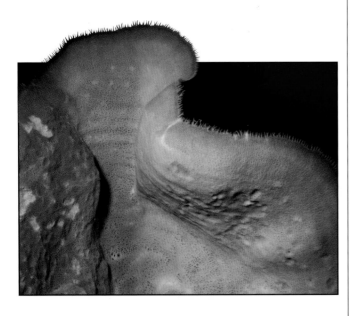

ELEPHANT'S-EAR SPONGE

This large tropical sponge grows upright in a wavy, curved, flaplike shape. It varies in color from bright yellow to deep orange and red.

Glass or siliceous sponges have tiny spikelike spicules made of silica, a see-through mineral similar to glass.

BARREL SPONGES

Some barrel sponges are big enough for a child to fit inside. However, the inner surface is often very hard and scratchy.

JOINED TOGETHER

Many sponges live crowded together with others of their own species. Some even merge their bodies together, so it is difficult to see where one individual ends and another begins. Encrusting sponges spread over rocks in this way, with new individuals forming as the sponge colony enlarges. Sometimes, several sponges in a group have their own inlet holes for water, but their hollow inside chambers all merge together, so that they all share one outlet hole at the top. Sponges also grow at different speeds. In very cold water, some only grow by $1/10$ inch (2.5 mm) every year.

SPONGES FOR SALE

Bath sponges are not living sponges but the dead remains of their "skeletons." Most bath sponges have a skeleton of strong, springy, stringlike fibers rather than sharp spicules.

The trade in bath sponges has put some species under threat.

MADE MAINLY OF JELLY

After the simplest animals, sponges, the next simplest creatures are in the phylum Cnidaria, literally meaning "stinging creature." This has 9,000 different species. Most are better known as jellyfish, anemones, and corals.

SNAKELOCKS ANEMONE

The polyp form of cnidarian, like this adult anemone, is usually attached to something and is hardly able to move around, if at all.

PURPLE-STRIPED JELLYFISH

The medusa or umbrella-shaped form of cnidarian, like the adult jellyfish (above), is generally free to drift with the currents or swim slowly using its own simple muscles.

MAIN TYPES

There are three main groups of cnidarians, which were formerly called coelenterates. One is the scyphozoans or "cup animals," the jellyfish. The second is the anthozoans or "flower animals," which includes sea anemones and coral creatures. The third is the hydrozoans, a name that simply means "water animals." Hydrozoans vary from tiny treelike creatures in ponds to massive jellyfish in the ocean.

TWO BODY FORMS

Cnidarians have two main body forms. The first is the medusa form of the jellyfish. This means that the animal has an umbrella-shaped main body and stinging tentacles that hang beneath it. The second is the polyp form. The body is below, usually tubelike in shape, with the stinging tentacles sticking up from it. Sea anemones and similar looking but smaller coral animals are polyps.

Some cnidarians do not quite fit into the main groups. Mushroom anemones are not real anemones. They are also similar to stony corals, but they are not in this group either. They have their own group, false-corals or corallimorphs, which means "coral shapes."

Elephant's ear false-coral is 12 inches (30 cm) across.

ONE AFTER THE OTHER

Some cnidarians have both the medusa and polyp forms, but at different stages in their lives. Jellyfish are polyps when very young. These develop into the familiar swimming or drifting adult forms, medusae. This happens with each generation, one after another.

Hydrozoans have more combinations of body forms. Some are small polyps when young and then medusae when bigger, while others are the opposite. Also, some polyp forms of hydrozoans look like medusae, while others are the other way around. Corals and sea anemones are usually only polyps, with no medusa stage.

CORAL REEF

Stony "skeletons" of coral are made by small coral animals, which are often called coral polyps.

OCEAN WANDERERS

Jellyfish drift through almost all the world's oceans, even the colder waters toward the far north and south. Most are at the mercy of the currents. Big storms may wash thousands of them onto the shore, where they dry out and soon die.

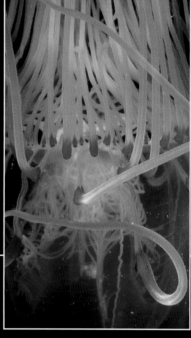

STINGS
Almost all jellyfish have stinging tentacles, but only a few have a sting powerful enough to harm humans.

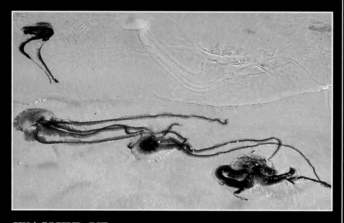

WASHED UP
Even as jellyfish lie dying on the beach, they can still give painful stings. They should be avoided or carefully buried.

POISONOUS HUNTERS
Jellyfish may not look like carnivores, but they are deadly hunters. Most of them catch their prey by stinging them with their long tentacles. Usually, the prey just happens to be passing by and brushes against the ends of the tentacles, which are difficult to see or detect in the water.

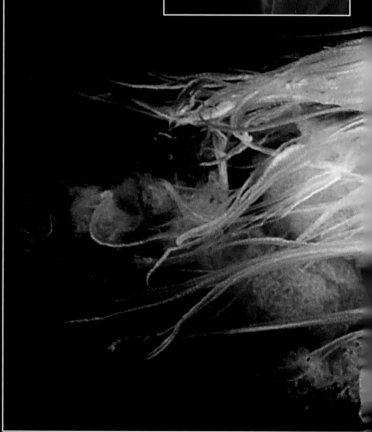

HELD FAST
The stings jab poison that paralyzes the prey and makes it unable to move. Then more tentacles curl around to finish the kill and drag the prey toward the jellyfish's mouth, in the middle of its underside. The largest mouth (oral) tentacles then help to push it in.

A BIG MEAL

Slowly the prey's body is digested by powerful juices in the jellyfish's stomach. Then any hard pieces and leftovers are "spit out" back through the mouth. A meal like a shrimp or small fish can feed a jellyfish for several weeks. Some jellyfish have short, thin tentacles. They "sweep" the water to grab floating pieces of food such as the tiny animals that make up plankton.

SWARM

Jellyfish may be swept together by currents into swarms. Often they breed at this time. They cast their tiny female egg cells and male sperm cells into the water, where they join or fertilize to begin new baby jellyfish.

DANGER! SEA WASP!

The sea wasp is named after its very painful sting. It is also called the box jelly because of its square-shaped body. It has four main tentacles, like many other anemones, with bands of stinging cells carrying nerve poison. In Southeast Asia and Australia, these jellyfish have killed many people, although there is an antidote against the poison.

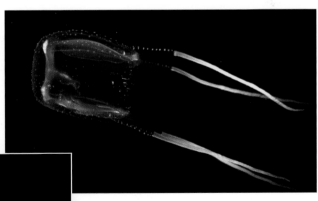

Sea wasp

LION'S MANE

The jellyfish (above) has a body of 3 feet (.915 m) across. Thin stinging tentacles hang from the edge of the bell, and four larger ones surround the mouth.

UPSIDE DOWN

The cassiopeia jellyfish (left) lives more like an anemone, upside down on the sea bed. It filters tiny pieces of food with its frilly tentacles.

21

TINY TREES TO BIG BUBBLES

The hydra is a tiny, treelike simple creature that lives in ponds. A man-of-war is a big ocean jellyfish with a bubblelike float and deadly stings. Yet both are members of the same cnidarian group, hydrozoans.

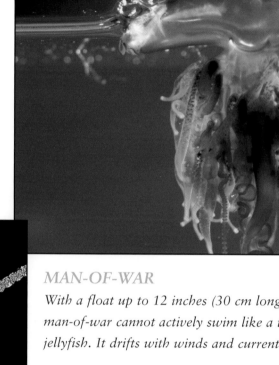

MAN-OF-WAR
With a float up to 12 inches (30 cm long) the man-of-war cannot actively swim like a true jellyfish. It drifts with winds and currents.

VERY VARIED
Most hydrozoans are quite small and for most of their lives they are polyps, like the pond hydra itself. Indeed some hydrozoans have no free-swimming, medusa stage at all. There are many kinds of hydras, living in fresh water and in the sea. Most are tiny, but some grow to be as big as a finger.

POND HYDRA
The green hydra of ponds and streams only grows as tall as this "l." It lives like an anemone, catching tiny pond life with its stinging tentacles. The hydra (above) has its young growing as a "bud" on its stalk.

HYDROCORALS
Some hydrozoan polyps build stony cups around themselves for protection. As these are added to over the years, they form branching shapes, just like real corals.

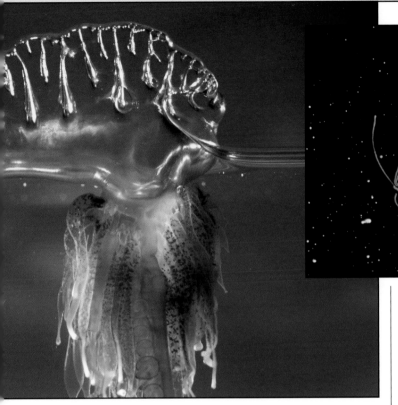

ONE ANIMAL THAT ISN'T...

Many hydrozoans live in groups. Some simply grow alongside others of their species. But some make up what looks like one much larger animal. The man-of-war consists of several sets of very different kinds of polyps. One is large and gas-filled and keeps the whole colony afloat. Digestive polyps just below it digest food caught by the stinging polyps that form the very long tentacles.

MULTI-COLONIES

The man-of-war is a member of the group called siphonophores. Most of these live in the open ocean as colonies that look like single animals. Some can even "pulse" like jellyfish to swim actively. Specialized polyps around the edge make these movements to propel the whole colony. The colony's thin tentacles make darting movements to attract fish, which think the tentacles are tiny creatures to eat.

DEADLY TRAP

The tentacles of the man-of-war, or bluebottle, can trail in the sea for more than 60 feet (18 m). The stinging polyps fasten onto prey such as fish with their tiny poison barbs. They then haul the victims up to the mouths of the shorter, tube-shaped feeding polyps, which then digest the meal. The resulting nutrients are spread and shared throughout the whole colony. Other frilly tentacles below the float are male and female polyps for breeding.

Another victim of the man-of-war

DEADLY STINGERS

Anemones are as beautiful as they are deadly. Nearly all live in the sea, although a few can survive in the part-salty water at the mouths of rivers. They sit on rocks, waiting quietly for prey to pass by, so they can stick on, sting in, and engulf their meal.

TENTACLES
The rounded blobs at the ends of these tentacles have many tiny stinger cells. They can release mucus, a sticky slime, to hold the prey and slow its movements.

PRAWN FEAST
Beadlet anemones can be many different colors, including red, green, brown, and orange.

SLOW SHUFFLE
Along with their close cousins the corals, anemones do not have a medusa stage in their development. They stick to hard surfaces like rocks or pieces of floating wood. However, many kinds are not completely fixed. The base of the stalk is a strong sucker and the anemone can slide or "shuffle" slowly away from danger.

MAKING MORE ANEMONES
Like many simple animals, anemones and other cnidarians breed in several ways. They can, like plants, form "buds" on their stalks that grow into new small anemones, which then glide away. If an anemone is cut into pieces, perhaps by a predator, then certain pieces can grow or regenerate into new anemones. This is called asexual reproduction. They also breed like other creatures, by eggs and sperm, which is sexual reproduction.

Some anemones (right) look so much like flowers that they are named after them. This dahlia anemone has its mouth open waiting for food, in the middle of the rings of tentacles, which can number more than 100.

Up to 12 inches (30 cm) high, some anemones (below) have thin tentacles on several wavy lobes above a narrow stalk.

OUT OF WATER

Many anemones live along the seashore and are exposed to the air at low tide. So they fold their tentacles inward and down and make their stalks much smaller and flatter. In this way, they are protected from drying out and from predators. They look like ordinary blobs of jelly on the rocks—until the tide returns.

ANEMONE WARS

Red beadlet anemones try for best sites.

Anemones can have fierce battles. Some places on a rock are better than others for catching prey or hiding from danger. To occupy these favored positions, anemones slide along and bump into each other, push and shove, and even lean over to sting each other. It is a continual struggle, although carried out in very slow motion.

25

Sea anemones are deadly to some small creatures, but great "friends" with others. They form partnerships with different kinds of animals and both sides benefit. Helpful relationships like this are known as symbiosis.

HERMIT CRAB AND CALLIACTIS
The calliactis anemone bends over to sweep up pieces of the crab's food, while the crab has a "hitchhiker" that hides it from its enemies.

WHY GET TOGETHER?
Anemones team up with many kinds of animals including fish, shrimps, prawns, crabs, and worms. In most cases, the other creature lives close to the anemone, perhaps under, or actually among its draping tentacles. Some creatures even stay right next to the anemone's open mouth! In general, the benefit for these creatures is protection and safety. Their usual predators avoid the anemone's stinging tentacles.

TUBE ANEMONE
Some sea amemones, like the one above, live in tubes made of leathery mucus to protect them from gritty sand grains.

CLEANER SHRIMP
Small cleaner shrimps pick up tiny pests and other bits and pieces from among the anemone's tentacles. The shrimp gets a meal from these bits, and the anemone is kept clean.

CLOWNFISH ON GUARD

In warm shallow seas, brightly colored clownfish nestle within the deadly "arms" of their friendly anemone. The anemone benefits because the fish chase away creatures who might try to nibble at their host. In turn, its clownfish lodger enjoys a warm and safe place to live where it can lay its eggs and rear its young.

The clownfish is immune to anemone stings.

PARENTING

Some anemones offer their offspring a very simple form of parental care. The young stay nearby at first and then grab any pieces of food that the adult rejects as being too small.

REEF PEST

Far from being helpful, the aiptasia anemone can become a pest on reefs. It is aggressive and breeds quickly. This pushes out other anemones and upsets the balance of life.

FAIR EXCHANGE

How else does the anemone gain? In some cases, its partner can be "bait." Its presence and movements lure other creatures who wish to eat it but are not experienced enough to know about the anemone's poisonous stings. So they come near to catch a meal—and become one themselves. The anemone may gain small bits of nourishment when its partner traps its own food, and the partner may gain food from the anemone in the same way.

LONG-TIME PARTNERS

But why does the anemone not catch and eat its partner, as it would a normal victim? In many cases the partner has a body covering of special mucus. This slime is exactly suited to protecting the partner against the stings. Also the slime may contain chemical substances that prevent the anemone's sting cells from being fired. Symbiotic relationships like this have taken a very long time to gradually evolve, one step at a time.

FANS AND PENS

Some types of anemones are far from alone. They live with others of their species in colonies on the seabed and form beautiful shapes like fans and feathers.

OLD NAME

Sea pens look like feathers and were named long ago when many people wrote using quill pens made from bird feathers. The sea pens are colonial anemones where, usually, one polyp forms the central rodlike shaft, or axis, and others branch away from it.

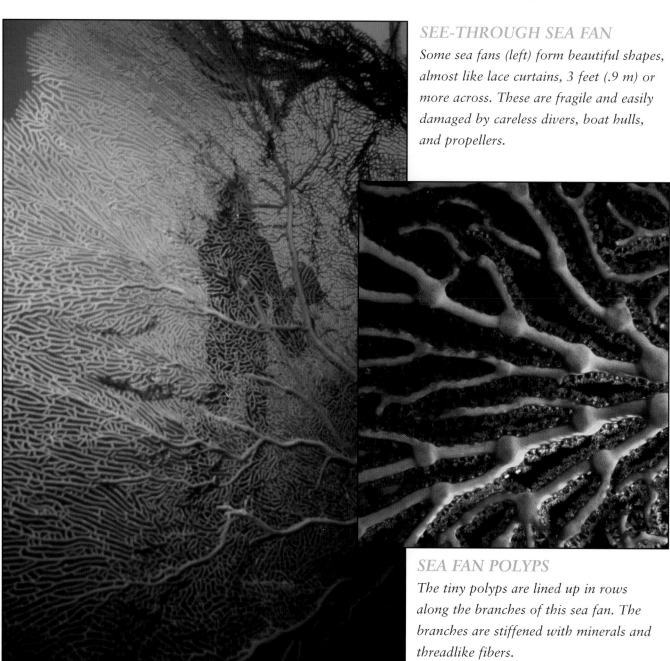

SEE-THROUGH SEA FAN

Some sea fans (left) form beautiful shapes, almost like lace curtains, 3 feet (.9 m) or more across. These are fragile and easily damaged by careless divers, boat hulls, and propellers.

SEA FAN POLYPS

The tiny polyps are lined up in rows along the branches of this sea fan. The branches are stiffened with minerals and threadlike fibers.

SLOW-MOTION PREDATOR

Sea pens are at risk from several predators, including the sea slug or nudibranch called tritonia. This crawls slowly along the branches consuming the polyps, unaffected by their stings. It can grow up to 12 inches (30 cm) long.

Tritonia

SPECIALIZED TASKS

The long, stiff axial polyp holds the whole colony clear of the bottom. Further specialized individuals, called lateral polyps, form the main side branches. These may be in a row or divided.

Sea pens and sea fans occur in all but the coldest seas. The polyps lining the side branches look like normal sea anemones and catch food in the usual way, with their stinging tentacles. They digest their small meals and the nutrients seep through the whole colony. In some sea pens, there are extra kinds of specialized polyps. These wave their tentacles and pulse their bodies to make water flow past. This brings more food to the colony, rather than relying on the sea's own tides and currents.

FLESHY SEA PEN

Like many other cnidarians, some sea pens have simple muscle and nerve fibers. When touched, they curl up for protection.

29

People have built many huge structures, from skyscrapers to bridges and sports arenas. But these cannot compare to the giant constructions of tiny coral creatures.

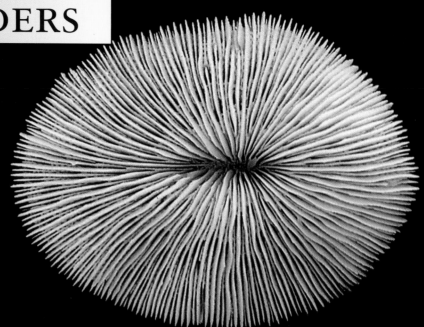

THE CORAL POLYP
A basic coral animal or polyp is very similar to a small sea anemone. It has a stalk or column as a main body and is fixed down at its base. Around the mouth at the top are many waving tentacles, armed with stings and poison. Most coral polyps are just one or a few millimeters tall, although some can grow up to an inch (2.5 cm) long. They catch tiny prey from the sea water flowing past.

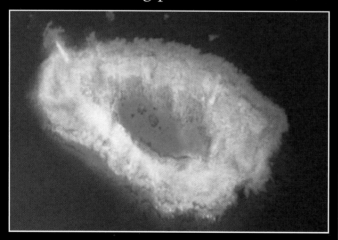

CORAL ATOLL
An island atoll is the tip of an undersea mountain that has gradually sunk, while corals have built up a ring shaped reef to stay near to the surface.

SKELETON SHAPES
Types of corals are often named after familiar objects, like mushroom coral. This is the dead, empty skeleton or framework of the colony.

CORAL SKELETONS
A key feature of most coral polyps is that each makes a "skeleton." This can be shaped like a bowl, cup, or tube, and is open at the top. The skeleton is built from minerals found in seawater, such as calcium carbonate. Other polyps make skeletons of strong fibers that are stiff or bendy like rubber.

SPAWNING
Like many simple animals, corals can breed asexually by budding. This is usually how they form their colonies ❶ . Or they can reproduce sexually by making tiny eggs (female) and sperm (male). The sperm and eggs are released at a certain time, often linked to the season and tide ❷ . They form a "cloud" that floats in the water as part of the micro-plankton "soup" of tiny living things ❸ .

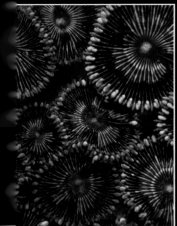

READY TO FEED

Coral polyps extend their tentacles around their mouths, ready to grab tiny pieces of floating food. Each is in a cuplike skeleton of stony minerals.

GREEN GUESTS

Many coral polyps contain tiny plants called algae. The polyps give the algae shelter and raw materials for food. The algae use sunlight to make the food, which the polyps eat.

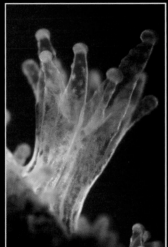

The brightly colored jewel anemone is not a true anemone, but a close cousin—a type of coral. It lacks any form of hard skeleton. As it makes more of its kind by budding, dozens and hundreds spread to cover the rock like a frilly blanket.

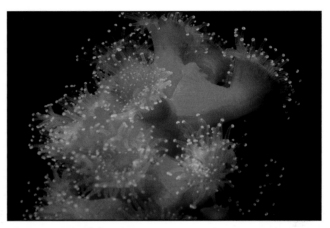

Corynactis californica

CORAL COLONIES

The skeleton gives its coral polyp support and protection. Most polyps live together closely in colonies with others of their kind. Their skeletons merge together to form larger lumps. Often times, their bodies are joined through holes, or channels, in their skeletons so the polyps can share food around the colony.

GROWING SHAPES

As the polyps breed, more add their skeletons to the overall colony. This happens in a certain pattern for each kind of coral. As polyps die, new ones grow on top of their empty skeletons. The colony's pattern of growth gradually builds up a large piece of solid material that resembles rock.

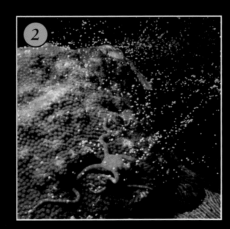

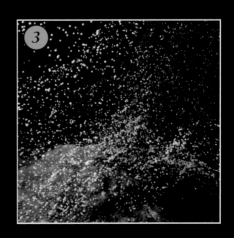

31

GLORIES OF THE REEF

Over thousands of years, millions of tiny coral polyps have built the largest objects made by any living things. These are coral reefs, and they are some of the richest, busiest, and most colorful places on Earth for wildlife.

WHERE DO REEFS GROW?

Corals grow best in warm, shallow, and clear water where the currents bring plenty of food and dissolved minerals. Many corals have algae growing inside their bodies as helpful partners in a symbiotic relationship. The algae need sunlight to thrive, and the corals cannot grow where the water is too murky, deep, or dark.

Most coral reefs are along the shorelines and around the islands of tropical and subtropical seas. The water here stays warm all year, usually within the temperature range of 72 to 82°F (22 to 28°C).

BRAIN CORAL

In this coral, the polyps form wavy lines that look like the surface of the human brain.

SOFT CORALS

These corals do not have hard, stony skeletons. Instead, like sponges, they are supported and strengthened by tiny spikes or spicules of minerals that are scattered through the colony.

OVERHANGS

An eel, octopus, crab, or lobster may make its home (lair) under a coral overhang.

SPEED OF GROWTH

Some corals get bigger by just a millimeter or two each year. Others can enlarge 10 times as fast, depending on the amount of food and the weather conditions. They may even grow on and encase shellfish such as giant clams (right). A powerful storm's waves can smash corals, leaving jagged remains that are gradually repaired.

Trapped giant clams

DAY AND NIGHT

By day many polyps (left) withdraw and the coral surface looks dull. At night they re-emerge and the reef glows with color again.

FANTASTIC HABITAT

Coral reefs are built from hundreds of thousands of coral colonies. Their skeletons grow, spread, merge, become covered, break off, and wear down. This forms a vast array of rocky crags, cracks, crevices, and caves. Fish, crabs, shrimps, octopuses, and countless other creatures, including simple animals like sponges and anemones, live in and around the reef.

ELK-HORN CORAL

A coral colony is shaped by its own growth pattern and water currents. However, regular nibblings by coral-feeding fish, urchins, starfish, and sea slugs also change the colony's appearance.

REEF IN DANGER

Coral reefs are very rich habitats, but they are also very fragile. They face many threats in today's world, and some are already gone forever.

PHYSICAL DAMAGE

Many coral colonies make hard, rigid skeletons. These can snap under the force of storm waves. They are also broken by boat hulls and smashed by their propellers. Snorkelers and scuba divers also rub and knock corals, by accident or through carelessness.

STORM DAMAGE

Big waves and strong currents are natural hazards for corals. Slim, branching types like elk-horn coral are especially at risk.

ACCIDENTS

This brain coral took perhaps 100 years to grow. But it has been smashed apart in a couple of seconds by a passing ship.

POLLUTION

Some coral reefs are on coasts near the mouths of large rivers. The river water carries mud, silt, and other particles out to sea. It also brings waste chemicals from factories along its banks, and pesticides washed from farm fields by rain. The particles smother the tiny coral animals and the chemicals poison them.

BLEACHING

A great crisis facing people and wildlife is global warming. A rise in sea temperatures of just a degree or two can have severe effects on coral life. The polyps die and the skeletons are "bleached" pale. Yet sometimes, they can recover.

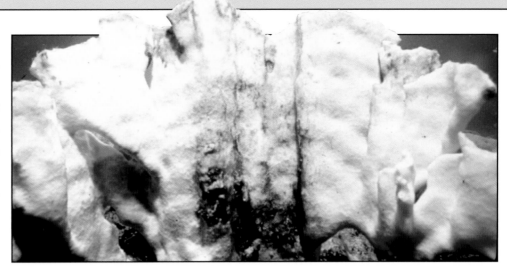

PRICKLY PREDATOR

The poisonous, well-protected crown-of-thorns starfish grows to 16 inches (40 cm) across. In the 1970s and 1980s, it greatly damaged the biggest reef of all— Australia's Great Barrier Reef.

NATURAL CHANGES?

Coral animals are eaten by many fish and other creatures. The crown-of-thorns starfish is a well-known "polyp predator" in the Indian and West Pacific oceans. Now and again, its numbers increase and it destroys huge areas of reef. This may be a natural process or cycle that has been going on for thousands of years, and the corals may recover. But human activities could be upsetting this delicate balance.

ARTIFICIAL REEFS

Sometimes old or damaged parts of reefs can be repaired by sinking cleaned objects like old metal girders and concrete bars. These form hard surfaces where corals can settle and start to grow into new colonies. Gradually a new reef forms, and the fish and other swimming creatures return.

An artificial reef made from concrete pipes

GHOSTLY CATCHERS

Comb jellies may look like narrow-bodied jellyfish, but they are not cnidarians. They form their own group, the Ctenophora, with about 100 other species. These bloblike simple creatures swim in the open ocean and catch other animals as food.

SMALL AND BIG
Some comb jellies are hardly larger than apple pips, others grow to 3 feet (.9 m) long.

COMBS ON JELLY
Most comb jellies are shaped like balls, grapes, or sausages. Their bodies are mainly clear jelly, and curving around the sides are eight comb plates, which are rows of tiny hairs known as cilia. These beat in "waves" like rowing paddles to make the creature swim.

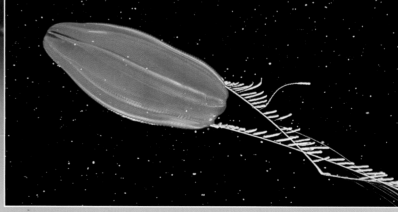

TRAILING TENTACLES
The comb jelly's two long tentacles usually have feathery side branches. These are covered with sticky substances that trap food.

RIPPLING COLORS

The beating of the tiny cilia hairs gives a rippling effect along the comb jelly's body. This produces flashing rainbow colors called iridescence in the dimness of the midocean water. By slowing the beating rate on one side of its body, the comb jelly can change direction, tumble, and twirl around.

A colorful comb jelly

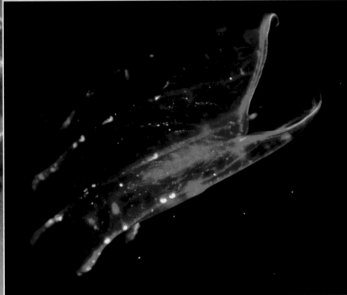

GLOW IN THE DARK

As well as their rainbow combs, many comb jellies can also glow in the dark. The light appears as faint pale streaks from the region of the eight pocketlike gut pouches inside the body. Living things that make their own light are called bioluminescent.

BODY AND TENTACLES

Each comb jelly has two long, sticky tentacles to obtain food. In the common comb jelly, the body is about 1 1/2 inches (3-4 cm) long, and the tentacles may be 1 1/2 feet (0.5 m) when fully extended. They are then pulled into pockets in the main body when not in use. The body has a mouth at one end and a light-sensing spot at the other. The main stomach inside has many pouchlike gut branches.

CATCHING FOOD

The comb jelly swims mouth-first and the tentacles trail behind like a long fishing net. Some comb jellies specialize in catching tiny prey like animal plankton. Others grab fish, squid, and other creatures, which may be almost as large as the comb jelly itself. The victim gets trapped in the sticky "net," then the tentacles shorten and curl around to bring the food into the mouth.

MOSS ANIMALS

On rocks, seaweed, pieces of driftwood, and even crab shells, patches of slightly fluffy-looking "moss" sometimes grow. But these are not plants. They are groups of tiny simple creatures called moss animals.

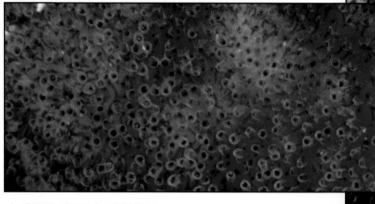

A CUP ON A STALK

Like ectoprocts, entoprocts (above) live in colonies. Each of these tiny animals has a cuplike head attached to a stalklike body. Hairs all along the edge of the cup trap its food. Unlike an ectoproct, the entoproct's mouth is also its anus.

VARIOUS NAMES

Moss animals have various other names, including ectoprocts and sea mats, because their colonies sometimes look like doormats draped over the rocks. They also form lacy patterns on seaweeds. Moss animals make up the main animal group Bryozoa, with more than 4,000 different kinds. Most live in the sea, but some are found in fresh water, from the bottoms of lakes to damp tree roots and gutters.

DIFFERENT INSIDE

Moss animals look similar to coral polyps, with a stalk that has a mouth on top and a ring of tentacles. But the tentacles do not have stingers, they have tiny cilia hairs to gather microscopic bits of food. Also, after digestion, a moss animal's food passes through a tubelike gut and the remains leave through a separate hole, on the side of the body. This is unlike anemones where the mouth is also the anus.

CRUSTS AND TUFTS

Each moss animal creates a strong boxlike container around itself for protection. The container, called the zooecium, can be made of either flexible fibers or hard minerals. The moss animal opens a door in it to poke out its tentacles when feeding. As moss animals breed they make new containers next to each other, and the colony spreads. Some colonies stay flat like mats. Others build up into lumps, grow in tufts like fluffy plants, or branch like bushes and trees.

GASTROTRICHS

These microscopic, wormlike simple creatures often live among moss animal colonies. They suck in almost any tiny piece of food.

BRYOZOAN "EGG"

Moss animals can breed to make large "eggs" called statoblasts. These have very tough outer cases and can float long distances. A statoblast (above) has an adult moss animal above it.

MESOZOAN MYSTERY

Mesozoans are very tiny, very simple animals that look similar to worms. Some kinds live inside bigger sea creatures like octopuses (left), starfish, sea snails, and ribbon worms. Mesozoans are parasites, stealing nourishment from their hosts. It is not clear if mesozoans are types of true worms or cousins of some other simple animal.

A host to mesozoan parasites

BEARS AND WHEELS

Two of the smallest and most curious kinds of simple animals are the rotifers, also called wheel animals, and the tardigrades or water bears.

TINY "BEAR"

Most tardigrades are smaller than the dot on this "i." Their closest cousins are certain kinds of worms.

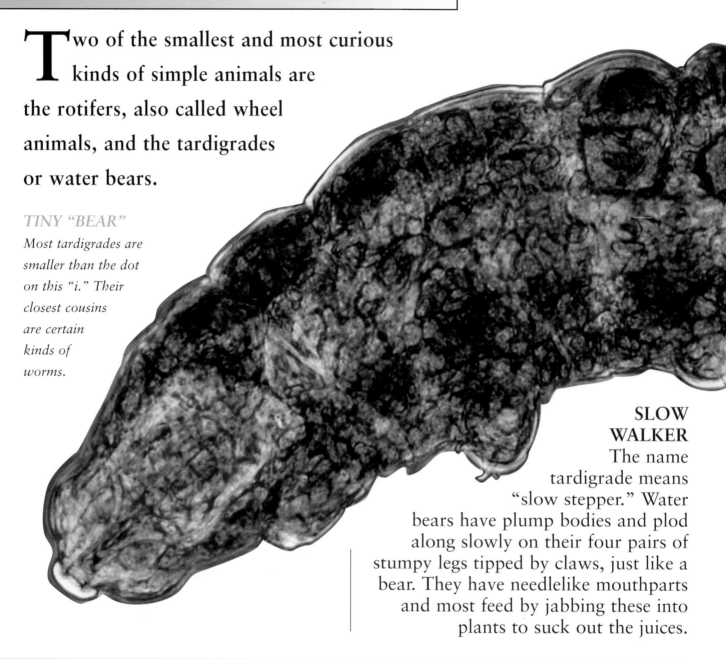

SLOW WALKER

The name tardigrade means "slow stepper." Water bears have plump bodies and plod along slowly on their four pairs of stumpy legs tipped by claws, just like a bear. They have needlelike mouthparts and most feed by jabbing these into plants to suck out the juices.

TOUGH SURVIVORS

Tardigrades can survive great heat and being dried out or frozen. They form a tough covering around the body and wait until conditions improve. They breed by females and males coming together to mate. The female molts or casts off her body casing, leaving the large eggs inside it (right).

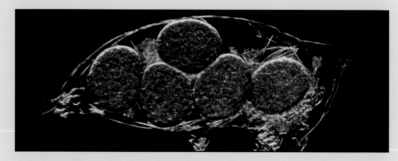

Eggs inside a water bear "shell"

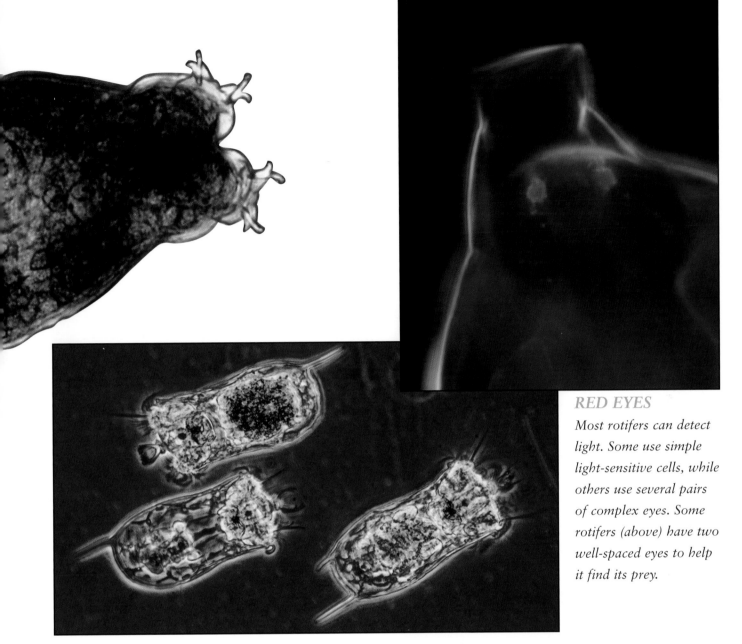

*Most rotifers can detect
light. Some use simple
light-sensitive cells, while
others use several pairs
of complex eyes. Some
rotifers (above) have two
well-spaced eyes to help
it find its prey.*

GRIPPING "TOES"

*Rotifers (above) have wheel-shaped crowns of hair, and
one or more short stumps at the other end with claws
to grip onto hard surfaces.*

WHEELY "HEAD"

Rotifers have bodies shaped like cups,
vases, funnels, balls, or tubes. At one
end is a double circle or "wheel" of
cilia. These beat to gather microscopic
particles of food and to make the rotifer
swim from place to place.

ALMOST EVERYWHERE

There are more than 600 kinds of
tardigrades and more than 1,800 kinds
of rotifers. Both are found wherever
there is water. Tardigrades occur from
the seabed to rain puddles, moist
soil, damp plants like mosses, and in
household gutters and rain barrels.
Rotifers are similar although they are
mainly freshwater. In both groups,
most kinds just look like tiny specks,
with the biggest being less than an inch
(2.5 cm) long.

BAGS AND BOTTLES

Some animals seem simple, yet they are close cousins of much more complicated creatures. The tunicates look like bags, but they have many similarities with fish.

STRANGE TADPOLES
The main animal group called tunicates contains about 2,000 different kinds of sea squirts and salps. Another name for their group is the urochordates. When they are young, they look like frog tadpoles. Each has a head end, a main nerve, and a stiff part along the body called the notochord. These are the same basic features found in young fish.

SALP CHAIN
Colonial salps link together as they waft slowly through the water. Like sea squirts and many other simple animals, they are hermaphrodites. This means they have both female and male parts for breeding.

BIG BAG OF WATER

A salp's body is hollow and mostly filled with water. The tiny cilia hairs inside beat and push water through, making the salp move along.

SIMPLER GROWN-UPS
The tiny "tunicate tadpoles" grow up to be adults that are much simpler, lacking any proper head end or main nerve. But the adults do have a heart and simple blood system, and senses to detect light, touch, and chemicals. All tunicates live in the sea. The sea squirts are attached to rocks or other hard surfaces, while the salps are pelagic, or free-floating.

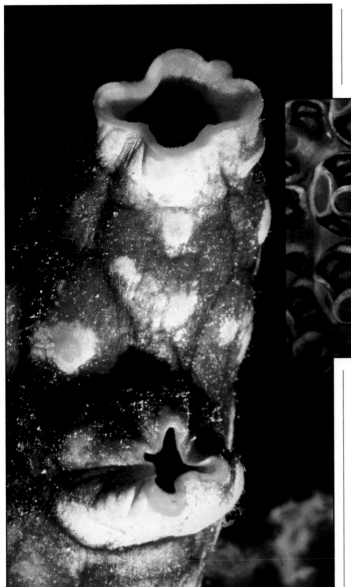

SEA SQUIRT COLONY

If a sea squirt is prodded or trodden on, it spurts out water, giving it its common name. Each larger hole is the intake hole for water (below).

STANDING TALL

Some sea squirts have stiff bodies and grow up to 2 feet (60 cm) tall. They may suck in and digest small prey such as shrimps and worms.

LEATHERY BAGS

Most sea squirts are shaped like vases, bottles, or bags. Their bodies are tough and leathery. Water is sucked in through a large hole at the top, filtered for food, and squirted out of a smaller hole at the side. The filtering hairs are often on the gills, which the sea squirt uses to take in oxygen from the water. Some kinds live alone, others form close-packed colonies.

CLEAR BOTTLES

Some salps look like glass bottles, while others resemble floppy plastic bags. Like sea squirts, they filter seawater for food using tiny cilia in the pharynx—a large hollow chamber inside the body. Water coming from the outlet hole at one end pushes them along. Individual salps may grow to more than 3 feet (.9 m) long. Some kinds form trailing colonies of more than 60 feet (18 m) in length.

BRACHIOPODS

Brachiopods, or lampshells, look very similar to shellfish, such as mussels, in the mollusk group. But brachiopods are very different from mollusks in the details of their body structure. This shows how looks can be misleading, especially for simple animals.

Fossil brachiopods

43

ANIMAL CLASSIFICATION

The animal kingdom can be split into two main groups, vertebrates (with a backbone) and invertebrates (without a backbone). From these two main groups, scientists classify, or sort, animals further based on their shared characteristics.

The six main groupings of animals, from the most general to the most specific, are: phylum, class, order, family, genus, and species. This system was created by Carolus Linnaeus.

To see how this system works, follow the example of how human beings are classified in the vertebrate group and how earthworms are classified in the invertebrate group.

ANIMAL KINGDOM

VERTEBRATE

PHYLUM: Chordata

CLASS: Mammals

ORDER: Primates

FAMILY: Hominids

GENUS: *Homo*

SPECIES: *sapiens*

INVERTEBRATE

PHYLUM: Annelida

CLASS: Oligochaeta

ORDER: Haplotaxida

FAMILY: Lumbricidae

GENUS: *Lumbricus*

SPECIES: *terrestris*

ANIMAL PHYLA

There are more than 30 groups of phyla. The nine most common are listed below along with their common name.

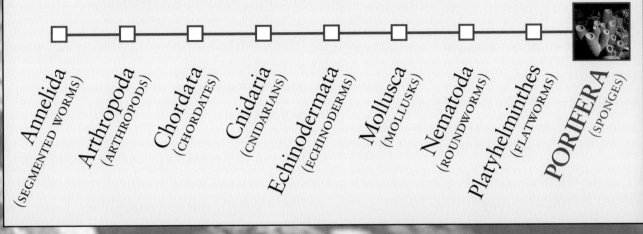

Annelida (SEGMENTED WORMS)

Arthropoda (ARTHROPODS)

Chordata (CHORDATES)

Cnidaria (CNIDARIANS)

Echinodermata (ECHINODERMS)

Mollusca (MOLLUSKS)

Nematoda (ROUNDWORMS)

Platyhelminthes (FLATWORMS)

PORIFERA (SPONGES)

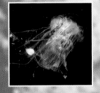

This book highlights animals from various phyla. Follow the example below to learn how scientists classify the *Aplysina lacunosa*, or the tube sponge.

INVERTEBRATE

PHYLUM: Porifera

CLASS: Demospongiae

ORDER: Dictyoceratida

FAMILY: Spongiidae

GENUS: *Aplysina*

SPECIES: *lacunosa*

Aplysina lacunosa
(tube sponge)

GLOSSARY

ALGAE
Very simple plants that do not have proper roots, stems, leaves, flowers, or seeds; however, they may have stemlike stipes and leaflike fronds and include most kinds of seaweeds

ASEXUAL REPRODUCTION
Breeding that does not involve female egg cells joining with male sperm cells

BIOLUMINESCENCE
When living things produce light perhaps to lure prey or to attract mates of their own kind for breeding

CILIA
Tiny short "hairs" that stick out from certain kinds of microscopic cells, and wave together like rows of tiny oars

EVOLUTION
The change in living things through time, as they become better adapted or suited to their surroundings or environment

EXTINCTION
When a certain species of living thing dies out, and the species can never come back

FLAGELLUM
A long, tiny hairlike part that sticks out of a microscopic cell, and that can be flicked or waved like a whip

FOSSIL
The preserved remains of an animal or an impression in rock made by the body of an animal

HABITAT
A particular type of surroundings or environment where plants and animals live, such as a desert, pond, or seashore

MEDUSA
A stage in the life of animals such as jellyfish, consisting of an umbrellalike body with a mouth in the lower center, surrounded by a dangling ring of long waving tentacles

MUCUS
A slippery, sticky, slimy substance made by many creatures, for example, to catch tiny food particles or to defend themselves against enemies

OSCULE
The main outlet hole or pore from a sponge's body, through which water flows away after being filtered for food

PELAGIC
Floating or swimming in the open ocean, rather than living near the shore or seabed

PHYLUM
A major group of animals or plants, and the next-highest level below the kingdom—the animal kingdom has more than 30 phyla, including sponges and mollusks

PLANKTON
Tiny animals and other living organisms that live suspended in seawater

POLYP
A stage in the life of animals, such as corals and jellyfish, consisting of a stalklike body with a mouth at the top, surrounded by a "crown" of waving tentacles

SPECIES
A particular type of animal

SPICULE
Tiny spikes, plates, or rods of hard mineral substances, that make up the "skeleton" of animals such as sponges

SYMBIOSIS
When two very different species live closely together, and both benefit from the partnership

Look for more Animal Kingdom books:

Tree Frogs, Mud Puppies & Other Amphibians
ISBN 0-7565-1249-2

Ant Lions, Wasps & Other Insects
ISBN 0-7565-1250-6

Peacocks, Penguins & Other Birds
ISBN 0-7565-1251-4

Angelfish, Megamouth Sharks & Other Fish
ISBN 0-7565-1252-2

Bats, Blue Whales & Other Mammals
ISBN 0-7565-1249-2

Centipedes, Millipedes, Scorpions & Spiders
ISBN 0-7565-1254-9

Dwarf Geckos, Rattlesnakes & Other Reptiles
ISBN 0-7565-1255-7

Snails, Shellfish & Other Mollusks
ISBN 0-7565-1613-7

Lobsters, Crabs & Other Crustaceans
ISBN 0-7565-1612-9

Starfish, Urchins & Other Echinoderms
ISBN 0-7565-1611-0

Nematodes, Leeches & Other Worms
ISBN 0-7565-1615-3

FURTHER RESOURCES

AT THE LIBRARY
Hirschmann, Kris. *Sea Anemones*. Detroit: Kidhaven Press, 2005.

Morgan, Sally. *Sponges and Other Minor Phyla*. Chicago: Raintree, 2005.

Sharth, Sharon. *Sea Jellies: From Corals to Jellyfish*. New York: Franklin Watts, 2002.

Tocci, Salvatore. *Coral Reefs: Life Below the Sea*. New York: Franklin Watts, 2002.

ON THE WEB
For more information on *simple animals*, use FactHound to track down Web sites related to this book.
1. Go to *www.facthound.com*
2. Type in a search word related to this book or this book ID: 0756516145
3. Click on the *Fetch It* button FactHound will find the best Web sites for you.

INDEX